I0490844

K. L. Bennett

SAVING MONEY WITHOUT SACRIFICING YOUR LIFESTYLE

K. L. Bennett

K. L. Bennett

Copyright © 2023 By K. L. Bennett

All Rights Reserved.

K. L. Bennett

DISCLAIMER

The information in this book is provided for general informational purposes only and is not intended to replace financial or investment advice. The author and publisher are not responsible for any losses, damages, or other consequences resulting from the use of this information. Readers are advised to consult with a financial advisor or other qualified professional before making any financial decisions.

K. L. Bennett

TABLE OF CONTENTS

- Chapter 4: Cutting Your Monthly Expenses
- Chapter 5: Generating Extra Income
- Chapter 6: Long-Term Savings Strategies
- Conclusion

INTRODUCTION

Why Saving Money is Important

Saving money is one of the most important things that anyone can do for themselves and their families. Whether you are trying to build an emergency fund, save for a down payment on a house, or plan for your retirement, having money set aside for the future can help you achieve your goals and provide financial security. But why is saving money so important, and how can it impact your life? In this chapter, we'll explore the many reasons why saving money matters, and how it can benefit you in the long run.

At its most basic level, saving money allows you to have more control over your financial future. By putting money away regularly, you are building a safety net that can protect you in case of emergencies or unexpected expenses. This can include anything from a medical emergency to a car repair to a job loss. Having a cushion of savings can help you weather these challenges without having to rely on credit cards or loans, which can lead to high-interest debt and financial stress.

Another important reason to save money is to achieve your long-term financial goals. This could include anything from buying a home to paying for your children's education to retiring comfortably. By setting specific financial goals and saving consistently towards them, you can create a plan that will help you achieve your dreams and build the life that you want.

In addition to these practical benefits, saving money can also have a positive impact on your mental and emotional well-being. Knowing that you have a solid financial foundation can help reduce stress and anxiety, and can provide a sense of peace and security. It can also help you feel more in control of your life and your choices, which can lead to greater happiness and fulfillment.

Of course, saving money is not always easy, and it can require discipline, sacrifice, and hard work. But the benefits are worth it. By prioritizing your savings and making it a habit, you can build a strong financial foundation that will serve you well for years to come. In the following chapters, we'll explore specific strategies and tips for saving money and achieving your financial goals.

The Myth of Sacrificing Your Lifestyle to Save Money

One of the biggest myths about saving money is that it requires sacrificing your current lifestyle in order to achieve your financial goals. This myth suggests that in order to save money, you need to give up the things that you enjoy and live a frugal, restrictive lifestyle. But this is simply not true.

In fact, the opposite can often be true: by saving money and making smart financial decisions, you can actually improve your quality of life and increase your happiness. This is because financial stress can be a major source of anxiety and unhappiness, and by taking control of your finances and building a solid financial foundation, you can reduce this stress and create a greater sense of peace and security.

One way to dispel this myth is to focus on the idea of "smart spending" rather than sacrifice. Smart spending means making deliberate, conscious choices about how you spend your money in order to maximize your happiness and well-being. This can include things like prioritizing experiences over material possessions, spending money on things that align with your values and passions, and finding ways to cut costs without sacrificing the things that you enjoy.

Another way to shift your mindset around saving money is to focus on the long-term benefits rather than the short-term sacrifices. This means recognizing that the choices you make today can have a significant impact on your future financial well-being, and that by making smart decisions and prioritizing your savings, you are investing in yourself and your future.

Ultimately, the idea that saving money requires sacrificing your lifestyle is a myth that can be dispelled with a little bit of creativity and intentionality. By focusing on smart spending, prioritizing your long-term financial goals, and making deliberate choices about how you use your money, you can build a solid financial foundation while still enjoying the things that matter most to you.

Of course, this doesn't mean that you should never make sacrifices in order to save money. There may be times when you need to cut back on expenses in order to achieve your financial goals. But the key is to approach these decisions with intentionality and purpose, rather than simply giving up things that are important to you without a clear plan or goal in mind.

In the following chapters, we'll explore specific strategies for saving money without sacrificing your lifestyle. These tips and techniques can help you find ways to cut costs, prioritize your spending, and build a strong financial foundation while still enjoying the things that matter most to you.

We'll start by looking at some of the most common areas where people overspend, and explore strategies for cutting costs without sacrificing your quality of life. This will include tips for saving on housing, transportation, food, entertainment, and more.

We'll also explore the concept of mindful spending, and how being intentional about your purchases can help you save money while still enjoying the things that matter most to you. This will include tips for avoiding impulse purchases, making smart choices about where you shop, and finding ways to get more value out of the things you buy.

Finally, we'll look at some specific strategies for building your savings and achieving your financial goals. This will include tips for setting realistic savings targets, automating your savings, and finding ways to increase your income.

Throughout the book, we'll emphasize the importance of taking a holistic approach to your finances. This means looking at your financial situation as a whole, and making deliberate choices about how you use your money in order to achieve your goals and live a fulfilling life. By following the strategies and tips outlined in this book, you can save money, build a strong financial foundation, and enjoy the things that matter most to you.

CHAPTER 1: ASSESSING YOUR CURRENT SPENDING HABITS

Tracking Your Expenses

Keeping track of your expenses is the first step to taking control of your finances. Start by gathering all of your receipts, bills, and bank statements.

Use a budgeting app or software to categorize your expenses into different categories like housing, transportation, food, and entertainment.

Set a budget for each category based on your income and expenses. This will help you identify areas where you may be overspending.

Make sure to track all of your expenses, including small purchases like coffee or snacks. These small expenses can add up quickly and impact your budget.

Review your expenses regularly to see where you can cut back. You may be surprised to find that you're spending more than you realized on certain categories like dining out or shopping.

Tracking your expenses can also help you identify areas where you may be able to negotiate better rates or find cheaper alternatives.

If you have a partner or family members who contribute to your expenses, make sure to include their income and expenses in your tracking.

Automating your expenses can also help you keep track of your spending. Use automatic bill payments and direct deposit to ensure that your bills are paid on time and you don't overspend.

Consider using a credit card that offers cash back or rewards for your expenses. Just be sure to pay off your balance in full each month to avoid accruing interest and debt.

Tracking your expenses can also help you plan for unexpected expenses like car repairs or medical bills.

Identifying Areas for Improvement

Once you have a clear picture of your expenses, you can start identifying areas for improvement. Look for categories where you're spending more than you budgeted for.

Determine whether those expenses are necessary or if there are ways you can reduce them. For example, you may be able to save money on transportation by carpooling or using public transit.

Look for subscriptions or memberships that you're not using and cancel them. This could include gym memberships, streaming services, or magazine subscriptions.

Consider downsizing your living space or finding a cheaper apartment or house. This can be a significant source of savings for many people.

Eating out and entertainment expenses can also be a source of overspending. Look for ways to save money on these activities by dining out less frequently or finding free activities like parks or community events.

Consider buying used or refurbished items instead of new ones. This can save you money on big-ticket items like furniture or electronics.

Shop around for insurance and utility providers to ensure you're getting the best rates. Don't be afraid to negotiate or switch providers if you can find a better deal.

Identify any bad habits you have that may be costing you money. For example, smoking, drinking, or gambling can all be expensive habits that drain your finances.

Look for ways to reduce your debt, including credit card balances and loans. High-interest debt can be a significant source of financial stress and drain your budget.

Finally, consider finding ways to increase your income. This could include asking for a raise, taking on a side hustle, or selling items you no longer need.

Setting Realistic Goals

Once you've identified areas for improvement, it's important to set realistic goals for yourself. This will help you stay motivated and on track.

Start by setting a specific financial goal, such as paying off your credit card debt or saving for a down payment on a house.

Break your goal down into smaller, more manageable steps. For example, if you want to save $10,000 for a down payment, break your goal down into smaller steps like saving $1,000 per month for ten months.

Set a timeline for each of your goals. This will help you stay focused and accountable.

Make sure your goals are realistic and achievable. If you set goals that are too ambitious, you may become discouraged and give up.

Write down your goals and keep them in a visible place, like on your refrigerator or in your planner. This will serve as a reminder of what you're working towards.

Celebrate your progress along the way. For example, if you've paid off a credit card balance, treat yourself to a small reward like a nice dinner or a movie.

If you find that you're not making progress towards your goals, re-evaluate your plan and adjust as needed. Don't be afraid to ask for help from a financial advisor or trusted friend.

Consider setting up automatic savings or debt payments to ensure that you're staying on track with your goals.

Finally, don't forget to enjoy the journey. Saving money and improving your financial situation can be a challenging but rewarding experience. Stay positive and focused on your goals, and you'll be on your way to financial success.

CHAPTER 2: CREATING A BUDGET THAT WORKS FOR YOU

How to Build a Realistic Budget

Start by tracking your current expenses. Before you can build a budget, you need to know where your money is currently going. Use a budgeting app or a spreadsheet to track your expenses over the course of a month.

Identify your fixed expenses. Fixed expenses are expenses that remain the same every month, such as rent or mortgage payments, car payments, and insurance premiums. These expenses should be included in your budget first.

Determine your variable expenses. Variable expenses are expenses that can change from month to month, such as groceries, dining out, and entertainment. Look at your spending habits and determine how much you typically spend on these expenses.

Prioritize your expenses. Once you've identified your fixed and variable expenses, prioritize them in order of importance. This will help you make decisions about where to cut back if necessary.

Set realistic goals. When building your budget, set goals for your savings and debt reduction. Make sure these goals are achievable based on your income and expenses.

Allocate money for emergencies. Unexpected expenses can derail even the best budget. Make sure to allocate money each month for emergencies, such as car repairs or medical expenses.

Use budgeting software. There are many budgeting apps and software programs available that can help you build and track your budget. Look for one that fits your needs and preferences.

Don't forget about annual expenses. In addition to monthly expenses, don't forget about annual expenses such as taxes, insurance premiums, and holiday gifts. Make sure to budget for these as well.

Revisit your budget regularly. Your budget is not set in stone. Revisit it regularly to make sure it's still working for you and make adjustments as necessary.

Seek professional help if needed. If you're struggling to build a budget or manage your finances, consider seeking help from a financial planner or counselor. They can provide valuable advice and guidance.

Tips for Sticking to Your Budget

Use cash for discretionary spending. Using cash for discretionary spending, such as dining out or entertainment, can help you stick to your budget. Once the cash is gone, you know it's time to stop spending.

Automate your savings. Set up automatic transfers from your checking account to your savings account each month. This will help you save money without even thinking about it.

Track your progress. Regularly track your progress toward your savings and debt reduction goals. This will help you stay motivated and focused.

Be realistic. Make sure your budget is realistic and achievable. If it's too restrictive, you're more likely to give up.

Find free or low-cost entertainment. Look for free or low-cost entertainment options in your community, such as parks, museums, and festivals.

Use coupons and deals. Before making a purchase, look for coupons and deals that can help you save money.

Cook at home. Cooking at home is typically much cheaper than dining out. Look for easy and inexpensive recipes to help you save money on groceries.

Avoid impulse purchases. Before making a purchase, ask yourself if it's really necessary. If it's not, wait a few days before making the purchase to see if you still want it.

Focus on experiences, not things. Instead of spending money on material possessions, focus on experiences that can provide long-lasting memories.

Don't be too hard on yourself. If you overspend one month, don't beat yourself up. Instead, use it as an opportunity to reevaluate your budget and make adjustments.

How to Adjust Your Budget Over Time

Evaluate your budget regularly. It's important to revisit your budget periodically to make sure it's still working for you. Evaluate your income, expenses, and savings goals to see if any adjustments need to be made.

Look for areas to cut back. If you're having trouble sticking to your budget or meeting your savings goals, look for areas where you can cut back. This could be anything from eating out less often to canceling subscription services.

Consider increasing your income. If you're struggling to make ends meet, consider taking on a side job or asking for a raise at work. Increasing your income can help you achieve your financial goals faster.

Factor in unexpected expenses. Even the best budget can be derailed by unexpected expenses, such as car repairs or medical bills. Make sure to factor in these expenses when creating and adjusting your budget.

Use windfalls wisely. If you receive unexpected income, such as a bonus or tax refund, use it to pay off debt or increase your savings rather than splurging on unnecessary purchases.

Revisit your savings goals. As your financial situation changes, so should your savings goals. Revisit your savings goals regularly to make sure they're still realistic and achievable.

Be flexible. Your budget should be flexible enough to accommodate changes in your income and expenses. Don't be afraid to make adjustments as needed.

Get creative. If you're having trouble cutting back on expenses, get creative with your solutions. For example, consider carpooling to save on gas or hosting a potluck instead of going out to eat with friends.

Don't forget about long-term goals. While it's important to focus on meeting your immediate financial needs, don't forget about your long-term goals such as retirement savings or a down payment on a house.

Seek help if needed. If you're having trouble creating or adjusting your budget, consider seeking help from a financial planner or counselor. They can provide valuable guidance and advice to help you achieve your financial goals.

In conclusion, creating a budget that works for you is an essential step in achieving your financial goals. By following these tips for building a realistic budget, sticking to your budget, and adjusting your budget over time, you can take control of your finances and work towards a secure financial future. Remember, it's never too late to start taking control of your finances and making positive changes in your financial life.

CHAPTER 3: MAXIMIZING YOUR SAVINGS POTENTIAL

Strategies for Saving Money on Groceries

Saving money on groceries is an important consideration for many households, especially in today's economy. There are many strategies that you can use to reduce your grocery bills and make your money go further. Here are some different ideas to help you save money on groceries.

- Make a grocery list before you go to the store. This will help you avoid impulse purchases and ensure that you only buy what you need.

- Shop for groceries on a full stomach. If you're hungry, you're more likely to make impulse purchases and buy things you don't need.

- Compare prices and shop around. Different stores may have different prices on the same items, so do your research and find the best deals.

- Use coupons and discount codes. You can find these in newspapers, online, and through loyalty programs.

- Buy in bulk. Buying in bulk can save you money over the long run, especially if you have a large family or if you eat a lot of a particular item.

- Buy generic or store-brand products. These are often just as good as name-brand products but cost less.

- Use cashback apps. Many apps offer cashback on grocery purchases, so be sure to check them out.

- Plan your meals for the week. This will help you buy only what you need and avoid wasting food.

- Buy seasonal produce. Seasonal produce is often cheaper than out-of-season produce.

- Use your freezer. Freeze leftovers and buy frozen fruits and vegetables to save money.

- Shop the perimeter of the store. The perimeter of the store often has fresh produce, meat, and dairy, while the center aisles have processed foods that can be more expensive.

- Don't shop when you're in a rush. If you're in a hurry, you may make more expensive purchases and not take the time to find the best deals.

- Use a rewards credit card. Many credit cards offer rewards points or cash back on grocery purchases.

- Use your local farmer's market. You may be able to find fresh produce at lower prices than in a grocery store.

- Buy in-season meat. Meat that is in-season is often cheaper than out-of-season meat.

- Use a grocery delivery service. These services can save you time and money by avoiding impulse purchases and providing access to exclusive deals.

- Avoid pre-packaged foods. Pre-packaged foods can be convenient, but they're often more expensive than making the same meal from scratch.

- Use store loyalty programs. Many stores offer discounts and rewards programs for frequent shoppers.

- Buy from discount grocery stores. Discount grocery stores often have lower prices than traditional grocery stores.

- Shop at the end of the day. Many stores discount items that are about to expire or that haven't sold during the day.

- Use your own bags. Some stores offer discounts if you bring your own bags.

- Don't shop when you're hungry. If you're hungry, you may be more likely to buy more food than you need.

- Buy store-made baked goods. Store-made baked goods are often cheaper than bakery-made goods.

- Buy generic medicine. Generic medicine is often just as effective as name-brand medicine but costs less.

- Use a price-tracking app. Price-tracking apps can help you find the best deals on specific items.

- Check the unit price. The unit price tells you how much an item costs per unit of weight or volume, which can help you compare prices between different sizes and brands.

- Use cash instead of credit cards. Paying with cash can help you stick to your budget and avoid overspending.

- Look for "manager's specials." Many stores offer discounts on items that are about to expire or that have cosmetic damage.

- Don't buy bottled water. Instead, invest in a reusable water bottle and fill it up at home or in public water fountains.

- Use leftovers creatively. Leftovers can be turned into new meals, reducing waste and saving money on groceries.

In conclusion, there are many strategies for saving money on groceries, ranging from making a grocery list and shopping around to buying in bulk and using cashback apps. By being mindful of your spending habits and adopting some of these strategies, you can reduce your grocery bills and make your money go further.

Finding Deals and Discounts

Use Coupons: Coupons are a great way to save money on groceries, household items, and more. Look for coupons in your local newspaper, online, or through loyalty programs offered by your favorite retailers.

Sign Up for Loyalty Programs: Many retailers offer loyalty programs that reward customers with discounts, cashback, and other perks. Sign up for these programs to take advantage of the savings and benefits they offer.

Shop at Discount Stores: Discount stores like Dollar Tree, Aldi, and Walmart offer low prices on a wide range of products. These stores often have their own brand of products that are much cheaper than name-brand options.

Use Cashback Apps: Cashback apps like Ibotta, Rakuten, and Dosh offer cashback on purchases made at participating retailers. Simply download the app, link your accounts, and start earning cashback on your purchases.

Buy in Bulk: Buying in bulk can be a great way to save money on everyday items like toilet paper, paper towels, and cleaning supplies. Look for bulk options at your local warehouse store or online retailer.

Follow Your Favorite Brands on Social Media: Many brands offer exclusive deals and discounts to their social media followers. Follow your favorite brands on social media to stay up-to-date on these offers.

Compare Prices Online: Use online shopping comparison tools like Google Shopping or PriceGrabber to compare prices and find the best deals on the products you need.

Wait for Sales: Retailers often offer sales during major holidays and shopping events like Black Friday or Cyber Monday. Wait for these sales to take advantage of deep discounts on the products you need.

Use Discounted Gift Cards: Sites like Gift Card Granny and Raise offer discounted gift cards to popular retailers. Use these gift cards to save money on your purchases.

Take Advantage of Student Discounts: Many retailers offer discounts to students with a valid student ID. Take advantage of these discounts to save money on your purchases.

Tips for Shopping Smart

- Make a List: Make a list of the items you need before you go shopping. Stick to your list to avoid making unnecessary purchases.

- Set a Budget: Set a budget for your shopping trip and stick to it. This will help you avoid overspending and stay on track with your savings goals.

- Avoid Impulse Buys: Avoid making impulse purchases by sticking to your list and budget. If you see something you want, wait a day or two before making the purchase to make sure it's something you really need.

- Shop with Cash: Shopping with cash can help you avoid overspending and stick to your budget. Leave your credit cards at home and only bring the amount of cash you need for your purchases.

- Look for Clearance Items: Many retailers offer clearance sections with heavily discounted items. Look for these sections to find great deals on the products you need.

- Use Price-Matching Policies: Many retailers offer price-matching policies that allow you to get the lowest price on a product. If you find a lower price at another retailer, ask your store to match the price.

- Buy Generic Brands: Generic brands are often much cheaper than name-brand options and can be just as good in terms of quality.

- Shop at Discount Stores: Discount stores like Dollar Tree, Aldi, and Walmart offer low prices on a wide range of products. These stores often have their own brand of products that are much cheaper than name-brand options.

- Don't Shop Hungry: Shopping when you're hungry can lead to impulse buys and overspending. Eat a meal or snack before you go shopping to avoid this temptation.

- Use a Rewards Credit Card: If you have a rewards credit card, use it for your purchases to earn points or cashback on your purchases. Just be sure to pay off your balance in full each month to avoid interest charges.

- Shop Online: Shopping online can help you save time and money. Many online retailers offer free shipping, exclusive online deals, and the ability to compare prices easily.

- Buy Used: Buying used items can be a great way to save money, especially for big-ticket items like furniture and electronics. Check out websites like Craigslist or Facebook Marketplace to find used items in your area.

- Avoid Brand Name Items: Brand name items can be much more expensive than generic or store-brand options. Look for generic or store-brand items to save money on your purchases.

- Use a Shopping App: Shopping apps like Honey and RetailMeNot offer discounts, coupon codes, and cashback on your purchases. Use these apps to save money on your shopping trips.

- Buy in Season: Buying fruits and vegetables that are in season can be much cheaper than buying them out of season. Look for deals on in-season produce at your local grocery store or farmer's market.

- Plan Your Meals: Planning your meals for the week can help you save money on groceries and avoid unnecessary purchases. Make a list of the ingredients you need and stick to your list.

- Buy Discounted Gift Cards: Sites like Gift Card Granny and Raise offer discounted gift cards to popular retailers. Use these gift cards to save money on your purchases.

- Use Coupons: Coupons are a great way to save money on groceries, household items, and more. Look for coupons in your local newspaper, online, or through loyalty programs offered by your favorite retailers.

- Shop at Farmer's Markets: Farmer's markets often offer fresh produce at lower prices than grocery stores. Check out your local farmer's market to save money on your produce purchases.

- Avoid Shopping During Peak Hours: Shopping during peak hours can be stressful and lead to impulse purchases. Shop during off-peak hours to avoid the crowds and save money on your purchases.

By following these tips, you can maximize your savings potential and still maintain your lifestyle. Finding deals and discounts, shopping smart, and being mindful of your spending can help you save money and achieve your financial goals.

CHAPTER 4: CUTTING YOUR MONTHLY EXPENSES

Saving Money on Utilities

Saving money on utilities can be a great way to reduce your monthly expenses and increase your savings.

One way to save money on utilities is to be mindful of your energy usage. Make sure to turn off lights and electronics when you're not using them.

Another way to save on utilities is to replace old appliances with energy-efficient ones. These appliances use less electricity and can save you money in the long run.

You can also save money on utilities by adjusting your thermostat. Try to keep your home a few degrees warmer in the summer and a few degrees cooler in the winter.

To save money on water bills, fix leaks as soon as you notice them. Leaks can waste a lot of water, which can quickly add up on your bill.

Use low-flow showerheads and faucets to conserve water and reduce your water bill.

Unplug appliances when you're not using them to save on standby power usage.

If you have a dishwasher, wait until it's full before running it. This can save water and electricity.

Consider using a clothesline to dry your clothes instead of a dryer. This can save money on your electricity bill.

Install weather stripping around doors and windows to prevent drafts and reduce your heating and cooling bills.

Use natural light instead of artificial light whenever possible to save on electricity.

Use a programmable thermostat to automatically adjust the temperature in your home when you're not there. This can save money on heating and cooling.

Take shorter showers to save water and reduce your water bill.

When washing clothes, use cold water instead of hot water to save money on your electricity bill.

If you have a swimming pool, use a pool cover to reduce water evaporation and save on your water bill.

Make sure your home is properly insulated to prevent heat loss in the winter and heat gain in the summer.

Use ceiling fans to help circulate air in your home and reduce your heating and cooling bills.

When cooking, use the smallest appliance possible and avoid preheating the oven. This can save on your electricity bill.

Turn off the water while brushing your teeth to save water.

If you have an old refrigerator, consider replacing it with a newer, more energy-efficient model. This can save money on your electricity bill.

Use a microwave instead of an oven whenever possible to save on your electricity bill.

Wash dishes by hand instead of using the dishwasher to save on your electricity and water bills.

Make sure your dryer vent is clear and clean to reduce the amount of time it takes to dry your

clothes and save on your electricity bill.
Use a low-flow toilet to reduce your water bill.
Plant trees or install shading devices to help keep your home cool in the summer and reduce your cooling bill.
Use a power strip to turn off multiple electronics at once when you're not using them.
Reduce the amount of paper you use by going digital whenever possible. This can save money on printing and paper bills.
Use a water filter instead of buying bottled water to save money and reduce waste.
Switch to LED light bulbs to save money on your electricity bill.
Consider carpooling or using public transportation to save money on gas and reduce your carbon footprint.

In conclusion, there are many ways to save money on utilities that can add up to significant savings over time. By making small changes in your energy and water usage, adjusting your habits, and investing in energy-efficient appliances, you can reduce your monthly bills and increase your savings. By being mindful of your utility usage and making simple changes, you can help protect the environment while also improving your financial situation.

Reducing Your Housing Costs

Reducing your housing costs can be an effective way to save money and improve your financial situation. There are several strategies you can use to lower your housing expenses, from negotiating rent to downsizing your home. Here are different ways you can reduce your housing costs and start saving money today:

- Negotiate your rent with your landlord. Many landlords are willing to work with tenants to lower their rent, especially if you have been a good tenant and have a good relationship with your landlord.

- Consider renting a smaller apartment or downsizing your home. If you don't need as much space as you currently have, moving to a smaller apartment or downsizing to a smaller house can save you money on rent or mortgage payments.

- Look for a roommate to split housing costs with. Sharing your home with a roommate can cut your rent or mortgage payments in half.

- Refinance your mortgage. Refinancing your mortgage can lower your monthly payments and save you thousands of dollars in interest over the life of your loan.

- Consider a shorter mortgage term. Choosing a shorter mortgage term can help you pay off your home faster and save you money on interest.

- Shop around for homeowner's insurance. Comparing insurance rates can save you hundreds of dollars a year on your homeowner's insurance.

- Consider a high deductible health plan. Choosing a high deductible health plan can lower your monthly premiums, freeing up money to put towards your housing expenses.

- Make energy-efficient upgrades to your home. Upgrading to energy-efficient appliances, windows, and insulation can save you money on your monthly energy bills.

- Use a programmable thermostat to save money on heating and cooling costs. A programmable thermostat can automatically adjust the temperature in your home based on your schedule, saving you money on heating and cooling costs.

- Cut back on water usage to save on your water bill. Taking shorter showers and fixing leaky faucets can help you save money on your monthly water bill.

- Use public transportation instead of owning a car. If you live in an area with good public transportation, using it can save you money on car payments, insurance, and gas.

- Negotiate your cable and internet bills. Many cable and internet providers are willing to offer discounts or lower rates if you negotiate with them.

- Consider switching to a cheaper cell phone plan. Switching to a cheaper cell phone plan can save you hundreds of dollars a year.

- Look for deals on groceries and household items. Shopping at discount stores and using coupons can help you save money on your monthly grocery bill.

- Use a budgeting app to track your expenses and find areas where you can cut costs. Many budgeting apps are free and can help you manage your finances more effectively.

- Rent out a spare room on Airbnb. If you have a spare room in your home, renting it out on Airbnb can bring in extra income to help you cover your housing costs.

- Install solar panels to save on your energy bills. Installing solar panels can reduce your monthly energy bills and save you money in the long run.

- Use a clothesline to dry your clothes instead of a dryer. Hanging your clothes to dry can save you money on your monthly energy bills.

- Shop at thrift stores and garage sales for furniture and home decor. Buying used furniture and home decor items can save you money on decorating your home.

- Cut back on eating out to save money on food expenses. Cooking at home can be more cost-effective than eating out.

- Cancel subscriptions and memberships you don't use. Review your monthly subscriptions and memberships to see if there are any you can cancel to save money.

- Use cashback and rewards credit cards to save on your purchases. Using a cashback or rewards credit card can earn you cashback or points on your purchases, which you can redeem for savings on future purchases.

- Use energy-saving light bulbs to reduce your electricity costs. Energy-saving light bulbs use less electricity and last longer than traditional light bulbs, which can save you money on your monthly electricity bills.

- Look for discounts and deals on home services. Many service providers, such as cleaners or landscapers, offer discounts and deals that can save you money on their services.

- Refinance your car loan. Refinancing your car loan can lower your monthly car payments and save you money on interest.

- Get a home energy audit to identify areas where you can save on energy costs. A home energy audit can help you identify areas where you can make energy-efficient upgrades to your home to save on energy costs.

- Consider a home equity loan or line of credit to consolidate debt. Using a home equity loan or line of credit can allow you to consolidate high-interest debt, which can lower your monthly payments and save you money in the long run.

- Use public libraries instead of buying books and movies. Borrowing books and movies from the library can save you money on entertainment expenses.

- Look for free community events and activities. Many communities offer free events and activities that can provide entertainment without costing you money.

- Consider refinancing your student loans. Refinancing your student loans can lower your monthly payments and save you money on interest.

Reducing your housing costs requires a combination of strategies that can be tailored to your specific situation. By implementing some or all of these strategies, you can lower your housing expenses and free up money to put towards other financial goals, such as saving for retirement or paying off debt. Remember that every dollar you save on housing costs is a dollar you can use to improve your financial situation, so take the time to explore your options and find the strategies that work best for you.

Downsizing and Simplifying Your Life

Sell items you no longer need. Go through your belongings and sell anything you no longer use or need. You can use sites like eBay or Facebook Marketplace to sell items online.
Declutter your home. Get rid of items that take up space but don't add value to your life. You'll have less to maintain and clean, and you may even be able to downsize to a smaller home.

Cut back on subscriptions and memberships. Review your monthly subscription memberships and cancel any that you no longer use or need. This can include gym memberships, streaming services, and magazine subscriptions.

Shop secondhand. Consider shopping at thrift stores or consignment shops instead of buying new items. You can often find great deals on gently used clothing and furniture.

Cook at home instead of eating out. Eating at home is often cheaper and healthier than eating out. Plan your meals for the week and make a grocery list to save time and money.

Buy in bulk. Purchasing items like toilet paper, paper towels, and non-perishable foods in bulk can save you money in the long run.

Use public transportation. Instead of driving everywhere, consider using public transportation to save money on gas and vehicle maintenance.

Walk or bike instead of driving. If possible, walk or bike to nearby destinations instead of driving. This not only saves money but is also better for the environment and your health.

Embrace a minimalist lifestyle. Living with less can be liberating and cost-effective. Focus on what truly adds value to your life and let go of excess possessions and obligations.

Create a budget and stick to it. Make a budget that reflects your financial goals and priorities and stick to it. This will help you avoid overspending and unnecessary expenses.

Use energy-efficient appliances. Replace old appliances with newer, energy-efficient models. This can significantly reduce your energy costs over time.

Use coupons and promo codes. Look for coupons and promo codes before making purchases online or in-store to save money on everything from groceries to clothing.

DIY instead of hiring a professional. Learn how to do simple home repairs and maintenance tasks yourself to save money on labor costs.

Rent instead of buying. Consider renting items like tools, equipment, and party supplies instead of buying them outright.

Reduce water usage. Turn off the faucet when brushing your teeth and install low-flow showerheads and faucets to reduce your water usage and save on your water bill.

Use natural cleaning products. Make your own cleaning products using natural ingredients like vinegar and baking soda instead of buying expensive commercial cleaners.

Negotiate bills and fees. Call your service providers and negotiate lower rates on bills and fees like cable and internet bills, credit card interest rates, and bank fees.

Buy generic instead of name-brand products. In many cases, generic products are just as good as name-brand products but are significantly cheaper.

Use a library card. Instead of buying books, movies, and music, use your local library card to borrow these items for free.

Stay informed about changes in your bills. Regularly review your bills and statements to make sure you're not being overcharged or paying for services you don't need.

In conclusion, cutting your monthly expenses can be a great way to save money without sacrificing your lifestyle. By implementing some of the tips and strategies outlined in this chapter, you can reduce your utility bills, housing costs, and other monthly expenses. From shopping secondhand to using energy-efficient appliances, there are many ways to reduce your expenses and live within your means. By creating a budget and sticking to it, you can achieve your financial goals and enjoy the benefits of a more financially secure future. So, take the time to evaluate your expenses and make the necessary adjustments to save money and live the life you want.

CHAPTER 5: GENERATING EXTRA INCOME

Starting a Side Hustle

Starting a side hustle can be a great way to supplement your income and pursue your passion at the same time.
Side hustles can range from selling goods or services online, freelancing, pet-sitting, or even starting a blog.

The first step in starting a side hustle is to identify your skills and interests. Think about what you're good at and what you enjoy doing in your spare time.
Once you've identified your skills and interests, research the market to see if there's a demand for your product or service.

Next, create a business plan outlining your goals, target market, and financial projections. This will help you stay organized and focused as you start your side hustle.

It's important to set realistic goals for your side hustle. Don't expect to make a full-time income right away. It takes time and effort to build a successful side hustle.

Networking is key to growing your side hustle. Join online communities and attend networking events to connect with potential clients or customers.

Use social media to promote your side hustle. Create a website, blog or social media pages to showcase your work and reach a wider audience.

Don't be afraid to ask for help or advice from friends, family, or mentors who have experience in the same field.

Consistency is key to growing your side hustle. Dedicate a set amount of time each week to work on your side hustle and stick to it.

Be willing to adapt and pivot if necessary. If you find that your original business plan isn't working, don't be afraid to try something new.

Use analytics tools to track your progress and make data-driven decisions about your side hustle.

Consider taking on freelance work to supplement your income while you're building your side hustle. This can help you gain valuable experience and contacts.

Look for ways to reduce your overhead costs when starting your side hustle. Consider working from home or using free tools and resources to save money.

Focus on providing excellent customer service to build a loyal customer base. Word of mouth is one of the most powerful marketing tools.

Don't neglect your full-time job while you're building your side hustle. Make sure to manage your time effectively and prioritize your responsibilities.

Set boundaries and prioritize self-care. It can be easy to burn out when you're juggling multiple responsibilities, so make sure to take breaks and practice self-care.

Take advantage of online learning opportunities to improve your skills and knowledge in your chosen field.

Consider partnering with other businesses or freelancers to expand your offerings and reach a wider audience.

Take advantage of free trials and discounts offered by online tools and services to save money while building your side hustle.

Stay organized by using tools like calendars, task lists, and project management software to keep track of your tasks and deadlines.

Invest in a good accounting software to help you manage your finances and track your income and expenses.

Build a portfolio or case studies to showcase your work and highlight your achievements.

Attend industry events and conferences to stay up-to-date on the latest trends and connect with other professionals in your field.

Use customer feedback to improve your product or service and make changes as necessary.

Don't be afraid to say no to opportunities that don't align with your goals or values.

Build a strong personal brand to help differentiate yourself from competitors and attract new clients or customers.

Keep an open mind and be willing to learn from your mistakes. Failure is a natural part of the entrepreneurial journey.

Celebrate your successes, no matter how small. Recognize and appreciate the hard work you've put in to build your side hustle.

In conclusion, starting a side hustle can be a rewarding and fulfilling experience, but it takes time, effort, and dedication to build a successful business. By identifying your skills and interests, creating a solid business plan, networking, promoting your brand, and providing excellent customer service, you can turn your side hustle into a thriving enterprise. Remember to stay organized, prioritize self-care, and be open to learning and adapting as you go. With perseverance and hard work, your side hustle can become a significant source of income and a gateway to a fulfilling career.

Freelancing and Consulting

Freelancing and consulting have become increasingly popular career choices in recent years. They offer flexibility, autonomy, and the opportunity to work on a variety of projects for different clients.

Freelancing involves offering services to clients on a project-by-project basis. This can include writing, design, coding, marketing, and many other skills. Freelancers often work from home or a coworking space and set their own schedules.

Consulting, on the other hand, typically involves offering expert advice and guidance to businesses or organizations. Consultants often have specialized knowledge in a particular industry or area of business and can help clients with strategy, operations, marketing, and other aspects of their business.

One of the main advantages of freelancing and consulting is the ability to work from anywhere. This allows professionals to live and work in any location, whether it's a big city or a rural area.

Another advantage is the ability to choose the projects and clients that you work with. Freelancers and consultants can often be selective about the work they take on, which can lead to greater job satisfaction and a better work-life balance.

Freelancers and consultants also have the potential to earn more than they would in a traditional job. Because they can set their own rates and work on multiple projects simultaneously, they have the opportunity to increase their income and build a diverse client base.

However, freelancing and consulting can also be challenging. These career paths require self-discipline, time management skills, and the ability to market yourself and your services effectively.

Freelancers and consultants also need to be comfortable with uncertainty. Projects can come and go quickly, and clients may have changing needs and expectations. This requires a flexible and adaptable mindset.

Another challenge is the lack of job security. Freelancers and consultants do not have the same benefits and protections as traditional employees, such as health insurance, retirement benefits, and paid time off.

To overcome these challenges, freelancers and consultants need to be proactive about managing their careers. This may involve networking, building a strong online presence, and continually developing their skills and expertise.

Freelancers and consultants also need to be proactive about managing their finances. This includes setting rates that reflect their skills and experience, creating a budget, and setting aside money for taxes and other expenses.

One of the keys to success as a freelancer or consultant is to specialize in a particular area. This can help you stand out from the competition and attract clients who are looking for your specific expertise.

Another important factor is building strong relationships with clients. This includes communicating effectively, delivering high-quality work, and being responsive to their needs and feedback.

Freelancers and consultants also need to be good at managing their time. This includes setting clear priorities, creating a schedule, and setting boundaries to avoid burnout.

When starting out as a freelancer or consultant, it's important to have a solid business plan. This should include a strategy for finding clients, setting rates, and managing finances.

One of the most important skills for freelancers and consultants is communication. This includes not only communicating with clients, but also with other professionals in your industry and potential collaborators.

Another key skill is project management. Freelancers and consultants need to be able to manage multiple projects simultaneously, meet deadlines, and deliver high-quality work.

Freelancers and consultants can also benefit from continuous learning and professional development. This can help them stay up-to-date with industry trends and best practices, and can also lead to new opportunities and career growth.

One potential downside of freelancing and consulting is the isolation that can come with working alone. To combat this, many freelancers and consultants join coworking spaces or attend networking events.

Another potential challenge is managing workload and balancing multiple projects. Freelancers and consultants need to be able to prioritize tasks, delegate when necessary, and avoid overcommitting themselves.

One advantage of consulting is the potential for long-term partnerships with clients. Consultants can work closely with a business or organization over a period of months or even years, providing ongoing support and guidance.

Another advantage of consulting is the opportunity to work with a variety of clients in different industries. This can provide exposure to new ideas and perspectives, and can help consultants build a diverse and interesting portfolio of work.

Freelancers and consultants also need to be aware of the legal and regulatory requirements for their work. This includes understanding tax laws, contracts, and liability insurance.

To succeed as a freelancer or consultant, it's important to have a strong work ethic and a commitment to delivering high-quality work. This includes being responsive to client needs, meeting deadlines, and going above and beyond to exceed expectations.

Freelancers and consultants can also benefit from building a network of other professionals in their industry. This can provide opportunities for collaboration, referrals, and mentorship.

One of the keys to success as a freelancer or consultant is to be proactive about marketing yourself and your services. This can include creating a website, building a strong social media presence, and attending networking events.

Another important factor is setting realistic goals and tracking progress. This can help you stay motivated and focused, and can also provide valuable insights into what's working and what needs to be improved.

Freelancers and consultants should also be aware of the potential for burnout. To avoid this, it's important to take breaks, prioritize self-care, and maintain a healthy work-life balance.

Finally, freelancers and consultants should be willing to adapt and evolve as their careers progress. This may involve learning new skills, exploring new industries, or pivoting to a different type of work altogether.

Overall, freelancing and consulting offer many advantages for professionals looking for flexibility, autonomy, and the opportunity to work on a variety of projects. However, these career paths also require hard work, discipline, and a willingness to adapt to changing circumstances. With the right mindset and approach, freelancers and consultants can build successful and fulfilling careers in their chosen fields.

Renting Out Your Property

Renting out your property, whether it's a spare room in your home or an entire vacation rental, can be a lucrative way to generate extra income. However, it's important to do your research and ensure you're following all legal and safety requirements.

Consider your target audience and the type of property you're renting out. Is it best suited for short-term vacation rentals, long-term tenants, or a mix of both? Identifying your target audience will help you determine your pricing and marketing strategies.

Research local laws and regulations related to renting out your property. This may include obtaining permits, collecting occupancy taxes, and ensuring your property meets safety and health codes.

When listing your property, ensure you have professional photos and a detailed description highlighting its amenities and unique features. Use online rental platforms or work with a property management company to maximize your exposure and reach potential renters.

Consider offering additional services or amenities to make your property stand out, such as a fully stocked kitchen or access to a pool or fitness center.

Maintain your property in top condition and ensure it's always clean and inviting for renters. This will help you attract positive reviews and repeat business.

Communicate clearly with your renters and establish clear expectations regarding check-in and check-out procedures, house rules, and any additional fees or charges.

Keep accurate financial records and separate your rental income from your personal finances. This will make tax season easier and ensure you're maximizing your profits.

Consider hiring a property management company if you're unable to manage the rental process yourself. This can help alleviate stress and ensure your property is always properly maintained and rented out.

Before renting out your property, it is important to understand the laws and regulations in your area regarding renting, as well as any tax implications.

You should also ensure that your property is in good condition and make any necessary repairs or upgrades before renting it out.

To find tenants, you can advertise your property on rental websites, through real estate agents, or by word of mouth.

When screening potential tenants, it is important to conduct background checks and verify their income and employment status.

You should also have a clear lease agreement that outlines the terms and conditions of the rental agreement.

As a landlord, you are responsible for maintaining the property and ensuring that any repairs are made promptly.

You should also be prepared to deal with any tenant complaints or issues that may arise during the rental period.

Setting a fair rental price is important to attract tenants and maximize your income, but it is also important to consider the local rental market and competition.

It is important to set aside funds for unexpected expenses, such as repairs or maintenance, as well as vacancies between tenants.

As a landlord, you should also have insurance to protect your property and liability insurance to protect against any accidents or injuries that may occur on the property.

You should also be aware of the laws regarding security deposits and ensure that you handle them correctly.

Communicating with your tenants and building a positive relationship can help ensure a successful rental experience.

It is important to respond promptly to any tenant concerns or issues and to keep the lines of communication open.

You should also be respectful of your tenants' privacy and avoid any unnecessary intrusion.

If you are unable or unwilling to manage the property yourself, you can consider hiring a property management company to handle the day-to-day operations.

A property management company can help you find tenants, handle maintenance and repairs, and collect rent on your behalf.

However, it is important to choose a reputable and trustworthy property management company and to clearly outline their responsibilities and fees in the contract.

Renting out your property can be a great source of income, but it is important to approach it as a business and to have realistic expectations.

You should also be prepared to handle any challenges or difficulties that may arise during the rental period.

When setting a rental price, it is important to factor in all of the expenses associated with the property, including mortgage payments, taxes, insurance, and maintenance costs.

You should also be aware of any laws or regulations regarding rent control or rent stabilization in your area.

When advertising your property, be sure to highlight its best features and amenities, such as location, size, and any unique or desirable features.

You should also be upfront about any restrictions or limitations, such as pets or smoking.

When screening potential tenants, be sure to ask for references and conduct background and credit checks to ensure that they are responsible and reliable.

You should also be prepared to negotiate with tenants on certain terms, such as the length of the lease or rental price.

It is important to have a clear and comprehensive lease agreement that outlines all of the terms and conditions of the rental agreement.

When collecting rent, be sure to establish a clear and consistent method of payment and to follow up promptly on any late payments.

As a landlord, it is important to stay up-to-date on any changes in the rental market or regulations that may affect your property.

Building a positive relationship with your tenants can help ensure a successful rental experience and may even lead to repeat business or referrals.

Above all, prioritize customer satisfaction and ensure your renters have a positive experience. Happy renters are more likely to leave positive reviews and recommend your property to others.

In conclusion, generating extra income is an important aspect of financial stability and can be achieved through various methods, such as starting a side hustle, freelancing and consulting, and renting out your property. Each of these methods requires research, dedication, and a strong work ethic to be successful. By following the tips and strategies outlined in this chapter, you can increase your earning potential and achieve your financial goals while maintaining your current lifestyle. Remember to always prioritize customer satisfaction and stay informed about any legal and safety requirements to ensure a successful and sustainable extra income stream.

CHAPTER 6: LONG-TERM SAVINGS STRATEGIES

Planning for Retirement

Retirement planning is essential for everyone, regardless of age or income level. The earlier you start planning for retirement, the better off you'll be when the time comes to retire.

The first step in retirement planning is to determine how much money you will need to live comfortably during your retirement years.
You should also consider factors such as inflation, healthcare costs, and potential changes in the economy.

One of the most important aspects of retirement planning is saving for retirement. You should start saving as early as possible and contribute to your retirement accounts regularly.

Many employers offer retirement plans such as 401(k)s or pension plans. If your employer offers one of these plans, it's a good idea to take advantage of it.
If you don't have access to an employer-sponsored retirement plan, you can still save for retirement by opening an individual retirement account (IRA).

It's important to diversify your retirement savings by investing in a variety of assets, including stocks, bonds, and real estate.
You should also consider the tax implications of your retirement savings. Some retirement accounts offer tax advantages, while others do not.

As you get closer to retirement age, it's a good idea to start thinking about how you will generate income during your retirement years.
Some people choose to continue working part-time during retirement, while others rely on income from investments or retirement accounts.

Long-term care is another important consideration in retirement planning. You should consider purchasing long-term care insurance to help cover the cost of any future care you may need.

Estate planning is also an important aspect of retirement planning. You should consider creating a will and setting up a trust to ensure your assets are distributed according to your wishes.

Social Security is another source of income for many retirees. You should understand how Social Security works and how to maximize your benefits.

If you plan to retire early, you should consider the impact of early retirement on your retirement savings and income.

It's important to regularly review your retirement plan and make adjustments as needed. Consider working with a financial advisor or retirement planner to help you create and manage your retirement plan.

Retirement planning is not a one-time event. You should continue to monitor and adjust your plan as your financial situation and goals change.

One of the biggest mistakes people make in retirement planning is not saving enough. Start saving as early as possible and contribute regularly to your retirement accounts.

It's important to consider the impact of inflation on your retirement savings. Over time, the cost of living will increase, so it's important to plan for this.

Healthcare costs can be a significant expense during retirement. Make sure you have a plan in place to cover these costs, such as purchasing long-term care insurance.

Social Security benefits are based on your lifetime earnings. Make sure you understand how your benefits will be calculated and how to maximize them.

It's important to have a diversified portfolio to help protect your retirement savings from market volatility.

If you have debt, such as credit card debt or a mortgage, consider paying it off before you retire. This will help reduce your expenses during retirement.

Retirement planning is a journey, not a destination. It's important to enjoy the journey and celebrate your progress along the way.
Consider downsizing your home or moving to a lower cost-of-living area during retirement to help reduce your expenses.

Consider working with a financial advisor or retirement planner to help you create a comprehensive retirement plan that takes into account all of your financial goals and needs.

If you're self-employed, consider setting up a solo 401(k) or SEP IRA to save for retirement.

Make sure to consider the tax implications of your retirement plan. Some retirement plans offer tax advantages, while others do not.

Consider your lifestyle and retirement goals when planning for retirement. How do you want to spend your retirement years?

It's important to have a plan in place for emergencies, such as unexpected medical expenses or home repairs.

Consider working with a financial advisor to help you create a retirement plan that aligns with your values and goals.

It's never too late to start saving for retirement. Even if you're starting late, you can still make progress toward your retirement goals.

Consider delaying Social Security benefits if possible, as this can increase your monthly benefit amount.

Consider your risk tolerance when investing for retirement. More aggressive investments may offer higher returns but also come with higher risk.

It's important to have a realistic understanding of your retirement income and expenses.

Consider purchasing an annuity to help ensure a steady stream of income during retirement.

Make sure to take advantage of any employer matching contributions to your retirement plan.

Consider using a retirement calculator to help you estimate how much you will need to save for retirement.

It's important to understand the difference between traditional and Roth retirement accounts, as they have different tax implications.

Consider working part-time during retirement to supplement your income and stay active.

Make sure to regularly review your retirement plan and adjust your investments as needed.

Consider working with a tax professional to help you maximize your retirement savings and minimize your tax liability.

Consider using catch-up contributions to help boost your retirement savings if you're age 50 or older.

It's important to have a plan in place for long-term care during retirement.

Consider setting up automatic contributions to your retirement accounts to make saving easier.

Make sure to have a plan in place for paying off any debt before you retire.

Consider working with a financial planner to help you create a comprehensive retirement plan.

Consider using a retirement income calculator to help you estimate how much income you'll have during retirement.

It's important to have a plan in place for withdrawing money from your retirement accounts during retirement.

Consider working with a financial advisor to help you navigate the complex world of retirement planning.

Consider using a target-date fund to help you manage your retirement investments.

Make sure to keep your retirement plan up to date as your life changes, such as if you get married, have children, or change jobs.

Consider using a financial planner to help you create a comprehensive retirement plan that takes into account all of your financial goals and needs.

It's important to have a plan in place for handling unexpected expenses during retirement.

Consider using a budgeting app to help you track your expenses and stay on track with your retirement savings.

Make sure to have a plan in place for estate planning and asset protection during retirement.

Consider using a financial advisor to help you create a diversified investment portfolio for retirement.

It's important to have a plan in place for managing debt during retirement.

Consider using a retirement income calculator to help you estimate how much you'll need to save for retirement based on your expected expenses and income.

Investing in Your Future

Investing in your future is a smart financial decision that can help you achieve your long-term financial goals.

The earlier you start investing, the more time your investments have to grow and compound.

There are many different types of investments, including stocks, bonds, mutual funds, and real estate. It's important to do your research and understand the risks and potential rewards of each investment before making any decisions.

Diversification is key when it comes to investing. By spreading your investments across different types of assets and industries, you can help minimize risk and maximize potential returns.

Consider investing in low-cost index funds or exchange-traded funds (ETFs), which can provide broad exposure to the stock market while keeping costs low.

It's important to have a clear understanding of your investment goals and risk tolerance before making any investment decisions.

Regularly review your investment portfolio and make adjustments as needed to ensure it stays aligned with your goals and risk tolerance.

Consider using a financial advisor to help you create a comprehensive investment plan that aligns with your financial goals and values.

Investing in a tax-advantaged account, such as a 401(k) or IRA, can provide significant tax benefits and help you save for retirement.

Consider investing in real estate as a way to diversify your portfolio and potentially generate passive income.

Don't try to time the market. Instead, focus on a long-term investment strategy and avoid making emotional investment decisions based on short-term market fluctuations.

Consider the impact of fees and expenses on your investment returns, and look for low-cost investment options whenever possible.

Avoid investing in individual stocks unless you have the time, expertise, and resources to conduct thorough research and analysis.

Be wary of investment scams and always do your due diligence before investing in any opportunity.

Finally, don't forget to invest in yourself. Consider investing in education and skills development that can help you increase your earning potential and achieve your long-term financial goals.

Creating a Plan for Your Financial Goals

- Creating a plan for your financial goals is essential to achieving financial success. Start by setting clear, measurable goals for your finances.

- Consider your short-term and long-term financial goals, such as paying off debt, saving for a down payment on a home, or building a retirement nest egg.

- Determine your current financial situation, including your income, expenses, assets, and liabilities.

- Develop a budget that aligns with your financial goals and values, and make sure to stick to it.

- Consider using a budgeting app or spreadsheet to help you track your spending and stay on track with your financial plan.

- Make a plan for paying off any outstanding debt, such as credit card balances or student loans.

- Consider using a debt consolidation loan or balance transfer credit card to help you pay off high-interest debt more quickly.

- Build an emergency fund to help you weather unexpected expenses, such as car repairs or medical bills.

- Consider setting up automatic contributions to your savings accounts and retirement accounts to make saving easier.

- Regularly review your investment portfolio and make adjustments as needed to ensure it stays aligned with your goals and risk tolerance.

- Consider using a financial advisor to help you create a comprehensive financial plan that takes into account all of your financial goals and needs.

- Make sure to have a plan in place for estate planning and asset protection, including creating a will and setting up a trust if necessary.

- Consider the impact of taxes on your financial plan and look for opportunities to minimize your tax liability, such as contributing to tax-advantaged retirement accounts.

- Consider purchasing life insurance or disability insurance to protect your family and your finances in the event of an unexpected illness or death.

- Don't forget to plan for the future by saving for major life events, such as buying a home, starting a family, or paying for college

- Stay up to date on changes in tax laws, investment trends, and other financial news that could impact your financial plan.

- Consider the impact of inflation on your financial plan and adjust your savings and investment goals accordingly.

- Regularly review and update your financial plan as your circumstances change, such as getting a new job or having a child.

- Seek out resources and education on financial planning, such as books, podcasts, and online courses.

- Remember that financial planning is a lifelong process, and staying disciplined and focused on your goals will pay off in the long run.

CONCLUSION

Recap of Key Strategies

- It's important to track your expenses and identify areas where you can cut back in order to save money without sacrificing your lifestyle.

- Creating a budget and sticking to it is key to achieving your financial goals.

- Finding deals and discounts is a great way to save money on everyday expenses, like groceries and household items.

- Downsizing and simplifying your life can help reduce your monthly expenses and free up money for other things.

- Generating extra income through a side hustle, freelancing, or renting out your property can provide an additional boost to your savings.

- Planning for your financial future, including retirement and other long-term goals, is essential to achieving financial security.

- Investing in stocks, bonds, and other assets can help you grow your wealth over time.

- It's important to keep learning and educating yourself about personal finance in order to make informed decisions about your money.

- Building an emergency fund can provide a safety net in case of unexpected expenses or emergencies.

- Negotiating bills and expenses can help you save money without having to sacrifice anything.

- Automating your savings can make it easier to save money consistently and avoid the temptation to spend.

- Prioritizing experiences over material possessions can help you save money while still enjoying life to the fullest.

- Choosing low-cost hobbies and activities can help you save money while still having fun.

- Staying motivated and accountable to your financial goals can help you stay on track and achieve success.

- Seeking the help of a financial advisor or planner can provide valuable guidance and support as you work towards your goals.

- Building a supportive community of friends and family who are also focused on saving money can provide encouragement and motivation.

- Avoiding debt and high-interest loans is key to achieving financial security and stability.

- Planning ahead for major expenses, like vacations or home repairs, can help you avoid going into debt.

- Focusing on your values and priorities can help you identify areas where you're willing to spend money and areas where you can cut back.

- Celebrating small victories and progress towards your financial goals can help you stay motivated and on track for the long term.

Maintaining Your New Financial Habits

Consistency is key when it comes to maintaining your new financial habits. Make sure to set realistic goals and stick to them over time.

Review your progress regularly to make sure you're still on track towards your financial goals.

Reward yourself for sticking to your budget and achieving your savings goals.

Identify potential roadblocks or challenges that could prevent you from maintaining your new habits and develop strategies to overcome them.

Seek out support and accountability from friends, family, or a financial planner as you work towards maintaining your new habits.

Stay motivated by visualizing the long-term benefits of your financial goals and how achieving them will impact your life.

Make saving and budgeting a part of your daily routine in order to make it a sustainable habit.

Focus on the positive changes that come with living a more financially responsible life, such as reduced stress and increased peace of mind.

Stay flexible and willing to adjust your habits as needed in response to changes in your income or expenses.

Find ways to make saving and budgeting fun and enjoyable, such as by gamifying your savings goals or competing with friends.

Keep learning and educating yourself about personal finance in order to stay informed and motivated.

Surround yourself with positive influences who support your financial goals and values, and avoid negative influences that might undermine your progress.

Learn from your mistakes and failures, and use them as opportunities to grow and improve your financial habits.

Don't be too hard on yourself if you slip up or have setbacks along the way. Remember that building new habits takes time and effort.

Practice gratitude and mindfulness as you work towards your financial goals, and appreciate the progress you've made so far.

Focus on the benefits of saving money, such as being able to achieve your dreams and live the life you want, rather than the short-term sacrifices you might need to make.

Be patient and persistent, and don't give up on your goals even if progress seems slow or difficult at times.

Remember that saving money isn't just about reaching a certain number or hitting a specific goal, but about building a more secure and fulfilling life for yourself and your loved ones.

Celebrate your successes along the way, and use them as motivation to keep going and reach even greater heights.

Finally, keep in mind that maintaining your new financial habits isn't a one-time accomplishment, but an ongoing process that requires commitment and dedication over the long term.

Continuing to Live Your Best Life While Saving Money

Saving money doesn't mean you have to give up the things you love or sacrifice your quality of life. In fact, it can help you enjoy these things even more by reducing financial stress and worry.

Look for ways to enjoy your favorite activities and hobbies without spending a lot of money, such as by finding free or low-cost alternatives.

Focus on building meaningful relationships and experiences, rather than accumulating material possessions.

Take advantage of the sharing economy and other innovative ways to save money on transportation, lodging, and other expenses.

Travel smart by planning ahead, choosing low-cost destinations, and using rewards programs and discounts to save money on flights and accommodations.

Practice mindfulness and gratitude in your daily life, and appreciate the simple pleasures that don't require a lot of money, like spending time with loved ones or enjoying a beautiful sunset.

Prioritize your health and well-being by finding ways to stay active and eat healthy on a budget.

Look for opportunities to give back to your community and make a positive impact, even on a tight budget.

Find ways to stay motivated and inspired by reading books, watching movies, or engaging in other forms of media that align with your values and goals.

Stay connected to your personal values and priorities, and make sure your financial decisions reflect these values.

Keep an open mind and be willing to try new things, even if they seem outside of your comfort zone or usual routine.

Embrace creativity and resourcefulness as you seek out new ways to save money and enjoy life to the fullest.

Invest in experiences and activities that will bring lasting joy and fulfillment, rather than temporary pleasure.

Seek out the company of like-minded individuals who share your values and goals, and who can provide support and encouragement as you work towards your financial objectives.

Remember that saving money is a means to an end, not an end in itself. It's a tool for creating a more fulfilling and meaningful life, not a restriction or limitation.

Stay positive and optimistic, and believe in your ability to achieve your financial goals while still living your best life.

Take care of yourself and prioritize self-care, as a healthy and happy individual is better equipped to handle financial challenges and make smart decisions.

Keep your eye on the big picture, and don't get bogged down by small setbacks or distractions.

Be flexible and adaptable, and be willing to adjust your plans and strategies as circumstances change or new opportunities arise.

Finally, remember that saving money and living your best life are not mutually exclusive goals. With the right mindset, habits, and strategies, you can achieve both and enjoy a fulfilling and financially secure future.

In conclusion, saving money without sacrificing your lifestyle is a challenging but rewarding goal that requires careful planning, discipline, and commitment. By following the key strategies outlined in this book, you can learn how to make smart financial decisions, build healthy habits, and continue to live your best life while saving money. Whether you're looking to pay off debt, build an emergency fund, or achieve your long-term financial goals, these principles and practices will serve as a valuable guide on your journey towards financial freedom and security. Remember, the path to financial success is not a sprint but a marathon, so stay patient, persistent, and focused, and celebrate every step of the way towards a brighter financial future.

www.ingramcontent.com/pod-product-compliance
Lightning Source LLC
Chambersburg PA
CBHW071113220526
45467CB00004B/1854